D1109715

ONE NATION FOR ALL
IMMIGRANTS IN THE UNITED STATES

LIFE AS AN INDIAN AMERICAN

ELLEN CREAGER

PowerKiDS press

Published in 2018 by **The Rosen Publishing Group, Inc.**
29 East 21st Street, New York, NY 10010

Cataloging-in-Publication Data
Names: Creager, Ellen.
Title: Life as an Indian American / Ellen Creager.
Description: New York : PowerKids Press, 2018. | Series: One nation for all: immigrants
in the United States | Includes index.
Identifiers: LCCN ISBN 9781538323380 (pbk.) | ISBN 9781538322420 (library bound) |
   ISBN 9781538323397 (6 pack)
Subjects: LCSH: East Indian Americans--Juvenile literature. | Immigrants--United States--
   Juvenile literature.
Classification: LCC E184.E2 C74 2018 | DDC 973'.04914--dc23

Developed and produced for Rosen by BlueApple*Works* Inc.
Art Director: T.J. Choleva
Managing Editor for BlueApple*Works*: Melissa McClellan
Designer: Joshua Avramson
Photo Research: Jane Reid
Editor: Marcia Abramson

Photo Credits: cover Pablo Rogat/Shutterstock.com, paul prescott/Shutterstock.com; title page Songquan
Deng/Shutterstock.com; flag Les Cunliffe/Dreamstime; background HorenkO /Shutterstock; p. 4 Dragon
Images/Shutterstock; p. 6 Rawpixel.com/Shutterstock; p. 8 Serban Bogdan/Shutterstock; p. 10 No 9 Army Film
& Photographic Unit/Public Domain; p. 12, 14 CRS PHOTO/Shutterstock.com; p. 13 Kamira/Shutterstock; p. 17
OFFICIAL LEWEB PHOTOS/Creative Commons; p. 18 wong yu liang /Shutterstock; p. 20 Milind Arvind Ketkar/
Shutterstock; p. 22 szefei/Shutterstock; p. 24 Asia Images Group/Shutterstock; p. 24 inset left stocksolutions/
Shutterstock; p. 24 inset right highviews /Shutterstock; p. 25 Paul Hakimata Photography/Shutterstock; p. 26
sirtravelalot/Shutterstock; p. 29 NASA/Public Domain

Manufactured in the United States of America
CPSIA Compliance Information: Batch BW18PK: For Further Information contact
Rosen Publishing, New York, New York at 1-800-237-9932.

CONTENTS

Chapter 1
WHO ARE INDIAN AMERICANS? 5

Chapter 2
HISTORY OF INDIA 9

Chapter 3
COMING TO AMERICA 15

Chapter 4
LIVING AS AMERICANS 19

Chapter 5
AMAZING ACHIEVEMENTS 27

Glossary 30

For More Information 31

Index 32

U.S. families with roots in the country of India are known as Indian Americans.

WHO ARE INDIAN AMERICANS?

An Indian American is a resident of the United States who was born in India or who is descended from parents born in India. Sometimes they are referred to as Asian Indian Americans so people do not confuse them with the indigenous peoples of North America, Native Americans. While all Indian Americans have roots in India, they come from many different religions, ethnic groups, regions, and economic backgrounds. Some Indian Americans come straight to the United States from India. Some come from other countries.

Many Indian Americans combine parts of Indian culture and American culture in their lives. Some hold on to cultural traditions and values from their homeland. These often include a reverence for their family, celebrating holidays such as **Diwali** (pronounced "divali"), cooking foods from their homeland, and valuing education.

Indian Americans are the most educated United States ethnic group. By age 25, about 73 percent have at least one college degree.

About 4 million people in the United States can trace their roots to India. That is about 1 in 95 Americans. The United States currently receives more legal immigrants from India than from any other nation. In 2014, 147,500 Indian immigrants arrived in the United States, even more than from China or Mexico. In 2015, the number of people living in the U.S. who were born in India soared to 2.4 million.

More than three-quarters of arriving Indian Americans are fluent in English, so language is not a barrier for their school or work.

Most Indian Americans are college educated and are able to find good jobs. Indian Americans work in all kinds of fields, such as business, science, engineering, medicine, technology, art, and politics.

Many Religions

Indian Americans practice many different religions. According to a study by the Pew Research Center in 2012, about 51 percent of Indian Americans are **Hindu**, meaning they practice the religion Hinduism. Many Indian Americans are Christian, Muslim, **Sikh**, or Jain. Some are Parsi, Buddhist, or Jewish. About 10 percent of Indian Americans do not practice a religion.

Hinduism was born in India in 1500 BC. It is considered by some to be the world's oldest religion. Its followers believe they live in a constant cycle of birth, death, and reincarnation, living many lives. They also believe in karma, which is the idea that your fate depends on your actions in life.

Buddhism was founded in India in the fifth century BC. Today, its leader, the 14th Dalai Lama, lives in India's Himalaya Mountains.

Christianity and Islam later came to India from other parts of the world. Through rulers and conquerors, they became part of Indian life and culture.

UZBEKISTAN
KRYGYSTAN
TAJIKISTAN

CHINA

AFGHANISTAN

PAKISTAN

NEPAL   BHUTAN

BANGLADESH

MYANMAR
(BURMA)

LAOS

INDIA

THAILAND

ARABIAN SEA

ADAMAN
ISLANDS
(INDIA)

NICOBAR
ISLANDS
(INDIA)

SRI
LANKA

INDIAN OCEAN

India is about the size of Texas,
California, and Alaska combined.

HISTORY OF INDIA

India is crowded. With nearly 1.3 billion people as of 2016, it is the second most populated country in the world after China. India has about four times as many people as the United States, even though India is only about one-third the size of the United States! Located in Asia, India is home to the famous Himalaya Mountains on its northern border with China, Nepal, and Bhutan. To the east are the countries of Bangladesh and Myanmar. To the south are the Indian Ocean and the country of Sri Lanka. To the west are the country of Pakistan and the Arabian Sea.

Nearly 4,000 years before explorers came to North America, the region that is now India had thriving towns and civilization. A series of rulers, conquerors, and conflicts shaped India over the centuries. One famous period of history was the Mughal Dynasty, which had its height of glory during the 1500s and 1600s. That is when India's most famous building, the **Taj Mahal**, was built.

As India became free, the last British ruler, Lord Mountbatten, and his wife met with Mohandas Gandhi (center).

Many European nations came to India in the 1600s to trade for textiles, spices, silver, and gold. Seeking economic control, the British Empire then took over India, pushing out the last Mughal emperor. Britain ruled India from 1858 to 1947. The Indian people protested against the British. The leader of the protests was Mohandas Gandhi. He believed that nonviolent resistance, called satyagraha, had the power to right wrongs and free the country from Britain's rule. He was right. In 1947, India got its independence from Britain. However, peace did not last. Gandhi was assassinated in 1948.

Fighting broke out between Hindus and Muslims. This split the country into two nations – the primarily Hindu India and the mostly Muslim Pakistan.

These upheavals caused many Indians to think of leaving their homeland for new countries in Asia, Europe, or North America. Many moved away.

However, laws in the United States were very strict. **Quotas** – numbers of immigrants allowed – meant that few Indians could emigrate there. In 1960, the United States had only about 12,000 Indian Americans. In 1965, when laws changed, many educated Indians began leaving India for the United States, a trend that continues even today. As of 2015, India had more of its people – 16 million – living abroad than any other nation.

Modern India is a peaceful parliamentary republic and growing world economic power. How bustling is modern India? It has five cities that are bigger than any city in the United States! Metropolitan Delhi had 24 million people in 2016, and Mumbai had 21 million. Other cities bigger than any in the United States are Bangalore, Chennai, and Hyderabad.

English is taught and spoken widely in India. Though British rule ended, the language stayed.

India is one nation, but it has 29 states, seven territories, and an estimated 600 districts. The main languages that children learn in school are **Hindi**, English, and their local language. Hindi is the most spoken, but there are 14 other official languages, including Bengali, Telugu, Marathi, and more. There also are an estimated 300 **dialects**, which further divide the languages

Lady Liberty

These days, few immigrants to the United States actually get to see the Statue of Liberty when they fly into airports across the country or come through land borders. Even so, the statue remains the most famous symbol of hope and freedom for new arrivals.

Located in New York City, the Statue of Liberty, or "Lady Liberty" as she is nicknamed, stands tall in New York Harbor. Her torch is held above her crowned head. She lights the way for America's newest people.

A gift from the French government in 1886, she is made of thin copper sheets over steel. Over time, the copper turned greenish-gray. On her pedestal is a poem by American writer Emma Lazarus that includes the famous lines "Give me your tired, your poor, your huddled masses yearning to break free."

In the early 1900s, most immigrants who came to the United States arrived by boat. They passed right by the Statue of Liberty to dock at nearby Ellis Island. There, they were processed before they were allowed into the country. Today, the Statue of Liberty still is a beacon for immigrants around the world.

The Network of Indian Professionals of North America is a nonprofit organization the creates a community for Indian American business people.

COMING TO AMERICA

At first, very few Indian American immigrants were allowed to move to the United States. A trickle of early immigrants in the 1800s was made up of farmers from India's **Punjab** region and other laborers. They came to America's unruly and wild West Coast to work on the railroads. Meanwhile, a few merchants made their way from India's West Bengal region to sell goods on the East Coast of the United States. Still, strict immigration rules and quotas kept most Indian people out. Many instead moved to other Asian countries or to Canada, Britain, Africa, or the Caribbean.

After India's independence in 1947 and the following violence and wars with new neighbor Pakistan, many dreamed of moving to the United States. For most, that dream had to wait until 1965, when the Immigration and Nationality Act was passed and laws changed.

Even then, the country only opened its doors to college students and workers who had skills and professions that the United States needed, and to a few Indian immigrants who had family in the United States. Most Indian immigrants, including those who were not educated or wealthy, were still not allowed to enter.

Between 1965 and 1993, nearly 559,000 Indian immigrants came to the United States. Most were well educated and middle class. Most settled in Indian communities in New York City, Chicago, Detroit, Washington, D.C., or Dallas. They brought their families, culture, and religion with them.

The Immigration Act of 1990 meant that even more Indian professionals in specialized fields like engineering and health care could come to the United States. Another wave of immigration came from 1995 to 2016 as high-tech and computer specialists arrived. That pushed the total Indian-born population to 2.4 million.

As a kid in India, Satya Nadella wanted to build things. He came to America for graduate school, and now he is getting his wish as the head of Microsoft, one of the world's most important tech companies.

Many early Indian immigrants adjusted quickly to their new home, but often experienced some culture shock. Many were in the highest and wealthiest class back home. They spoke English and were well educated. But in the United States, they were a minority group. They often experienced discrimination and prejudice. Over time, Indian Americans have had to overcome many obstacles in their new home.

Many Indian Americans have found success in the United States. The average income for a family of Indian immigrants is $103,000.

LIVING AS AMERICANS

Like other immigrant communities, the Indian American community is influenced by the cultures and traditions from their homeland and contemporary American culture. Here are some of the unique experiences of the Indian American community:

★ Making friends: Indian Americans often settle in cities and particular suburbs where there are other Indian Americans. Many then look to their local Hindu temple or cultural center to make friends and learn about local activities. In some communities, Indian Americans have started websites to let other Indian Americans in a particular city know where Indian groceries, dance lessons, wedding halls, or shops are. Some towns have newspapers just for Indian Americans.

Indian American weddings may include many colorful traditions, such as an exchange of garlands and vows.

Some Indian American business people have formed organizations, such as the Network of Indian Professionals, to connect with one another. People from a certain region of India often form an association. There are also Indian American clubs for social events or even for fans of sports like cricket, a favorite Indian pastime.

Indian Americans also make friends through work or in the wider community through their children's schools and neighborhoods. Extended families are often very close, and many Indian Americans also maintain strong ties with relatives back home. Some even take a 20- to 25-hour-long flight back to India every year to see family. They may stay for several weeks.

★ **Marriage traditions:** Arranged marriages are still common in India. Some young Indian Americans decide they would rather make their own decisions about marriage. Other young people still agree to have their marriage arranged.

In the United States, marriage ceremonies between Indian Americans can be lavish, elaborate affairs with traditional **sari** dress, jewelry, and **henna** tattoos. Sometimes, the groom arrives to the ceremony on a horse or elephant. When an Indian American marries someone who is not Indian, they may merge traditions from both of their cultures, or change the ceremony completely. For instance, instead of arriving on a flower-covered horse, the groom may arrive in a flower-covered classic car.

★ **Education:** Education is very important to many Indian American families. Every winner of the Scripps National Spelling Bee from 2008 to 2016 was an Indian American student! As in many cultures, parents may have very high expectations for their children's school achievements and behavior.

★ Gender roles: In many Indian societies, men have more power than women and act as the head of the family. Indian American immigrants may find that the roles of husbands and wives and daughters and sons change when they move to the United States. While gender inequality is also an issue in the United States, Indian American women may feel they have more freedom in the United States. Women in both countries continue to fight for gender equality.

★ Faith: Many immigrants find comfort in their local Hindu, Sikh, or Jain temples. Temples are not everywhere in the United States. They are usually clustered in Indian American communities. That is another reason Indian Americans often choose to live in those particular cities or suburbs.

Families celebrate Diwali night in the fall. They dress up and light many lamps and candles.

They Came from India

Yoga: This Indian spiritual practice has spread all over the world and in most every town in the United States. In the United States, yoga is a form of physical exercise with a meditation element.

Ayurveda: This ancient Indian form of alternative **holistic** medicine came to the United States in the 1960s and has since become popular with some Americans.

Bollywood films: Films from India regularly play at theaters in Indian American communities across the United States. Most of them are made by India's large film industry, called Bollywood.

★ **Holidays:** Once in the United States, Indian American families hold onto their holiday traditions. The most popular celebrations are Diwali and Holi. Diwali, the festival of light, involves plenty of joyful fireworks, food, gifts, and lighting of lamps and candles. Diwali is so popular in America that the U.S. Postal Service in 2016 issued a stamp honoring the holiday.

Holi, the festival of colors, celebrates the arrival of spring with the throwing of colorful powder, bonfires, parties, and games.

Indian cooking uses many delicious spices, such as cardamom, cumin, coriander, saffron, and turmeric.

★ Food: Indian restaurants have sprung up across the nation, familiarizing other Americans with delicious Indian foods like naan and tandoori chicken. Many Indian Americans shop at Indian grocery stores, which stock all sorts of ingredients not always found in American-based grocery stores, such as coconut water, red lentils, gourds called turai, tamarind paste, and 10-pound bags of basmati rice. Indian food also is slowly becoming available in big American grocery stores. Everyone likes naan!

Popular Indian American Foods

Samosa: vegetable or meat in a small triangle of puff pastry

Naan: puffy Indian bread

Tandoori chicken: spiced chicken roasted over charcoal in a clay oven

Mango lassi: an Indian smoothie with mangos

Butter chicken: chicken curry with mild spices

Biryani: mixed rice dish with spices, sometimes topped by meat

★ Fashion: Many Indian American women wear elaborate, beautiful saris and jewelry on formal occasions. Although some older Indian Americans wear saris every day, most younger women do not. Indian fashion has also spread to the wider American society. Henna tattoos, bangle bracelets, and the bright, flowing colors of Indian fabrics are becoming popular.

A Nation of Immigrants

Most Americans today can trace their roots to these 12 places, in order: Germany, Mexico, Ireland, United Kingdom, Italy, Poland, France, Puerto Rico, China, Norway, Netherlands, and India.

All U.S. citizens who are not descended from Native Americans are descended from immigrants. Today, Indian immigrants are one of the top groups moving to the United States.

THEN: In 1960, the largest foreign-born populations in the United States were Italians, Germans, and Canadians.

NOW: The largest foreign-born populations in the United States are Mexicans, Indians, and Chinese, according to most recent 2014 data.

AMAZING ACHIEVEMENTS

Indian Americans have made the most of the American Dream, with strides in medicine, science, high tech, arts, politics, and many other fields. Famous Indian Americans include:

★ **Indra Nooyi:** Chairman and CEO of PepsiCo. She was born in 1955 in Madras, Tamil Nadu, India. She came to the United States in 1978 for graduate school at Yale and then worked her way up the corporate ladder to reach one of the most powerful positions in American business.

★ **Nimrata "Nikki" Haley:** The former governor of South Carolina became the U.S. ambassador to the United Nations in 2017. Her Sikh parents emigrated from the Punjab region of India, first to Canada, then to South Carolina, where she was born in 1972.

★ **Sanjay Gupta:** The neurosurgeon and journalist at CNN was born in 1969 in Michigan. His parents emigrated from northern India in the 1960s and met in Detroit. His mother and her family were Hindu refugees from Tharushah, Pakistan, and his father's family was from Haridwar district of northern India.

★ Bobby Jindal: U.S. presidential candidate, 2016. His parents were immigrants from the Punjab region of India. They settled in Louisiana, where he was born in 1971. He served in the United States House of Representatives from 2005 to 2008, then as governor of Louisiana from 2008 to 2016. He was the nation's first governor of Indian descent.

★ Amar Bose: Acoustic engineer who founded the Bose Corporation; he also was a professor at the Massachusetts Institute of Technology. His father was a revolutionary who emigrated from the Bengal region of India to the United States in 1920. Amar Bose died in 2013 at age 83.

★ Aziz Ansari: Comedian, actor, and writer. His parents were immigrants from a Tamil Muslim family in Tamil Nadu, India. Ansari was born in 1983 in South Carolina. He has starred in "Master of None," "Parks and Recreation," and has made many other TV and film appearances.

★ Nina Davuluri: Miss America 2014. The first Miss America of Indian descent, she is a public speaker for diversity and civil rights. Her parents emigrated from Vijayawada, Andhra Pradesh, India in 1981. She was born in 1989 in Syracuse, N.Y.

Kalpana Chawla (center), one of seven astronauts lost in the Columbia disaster, was the first woman of Indian descent in space.

★ Kalpana Chawla: The first Indian American astronaut. In 1997 and 2003 she flew as a mission specialist aboard Space Shuttle Columbia. She died in 2003 when Columbia disintegrated upon re-entry to Earth.

★ Naeem Khan: The fashion designer has dressed everyone from celebrities to royalty. Born in 1958 in Bareilly, India, he moved to the United States in 1978 to work in the fashion industry in New York. His brand is now known worldwide.

These men and women are just a few of the Indian Americans who have helped make the United States and the world stronger, more prosperous, and more creative. What incredible things will the next generation of Indian Americans accomplish?

Glossary

dialect A regional version of a language with some different words and pronunciations.

Diwali Popular Hindu holiday, a festival of lights.

henna Vegetable dye used for body art.

Hindi The language most spoken in India.

Hindu The biggest religion among Indian Americans.

holistic Relating to something as a whole, such as the mind and body together.

Punjab Region of northern India from which many immigrants have come to the United States.

quota A limited number.

sari Many yards of silk or cotton cloth draped around the body, shoulder, and sometimes the head.

Sikh Person who follows the Sikh religion, which was founded in about 1500 in India.

Taj Mahal White marble mausoleum built in Agra, India, in 1631–53 by Mughal emperor Shah Jahan in memory of his wife.

For More Information

Further Reading

Demuth, Patricia Brennan. *What Was Ellis Island?*
New York, NY: Grosset & Dunlap, 2014.

Fleming, Candace. *Lowji Discovers America.*
New York, NY: Simon and Schuster, 2008.

Roman, Carole P. *If You Were Me and Lived in . . . India.*
Livermore, CO: Red Feather Publishing, 2014.

Smith, Robert W. *Spotlight on America:*
A Nation of Immigrants.
Garden Grove, CA: Teacher Created Resources, 2011.

Websites

Due to the changing nature of Internet links, PowerKids Press has developed an online list of websites related to the subject of this book. This site is updated regularly. Please use this link to access the list:
www.powerkidslinks.com/onfa/indianam

Index

A

Ansari, Aziz, 28

Ayurveda, 23

B

Bollywood, 23

Bose, Amar, 28

Buddhism, 7

C

Chawla, Kalapana, 29

D

Dalai Lama, 7

Davuluri, Nina, 28

Diwali, 5, 22, 23

G

Gupta, Sanjay, 27

H

Haley, Nikki, 27

henna, 21, 25

Hindu, 7, 11, 19, 22, 27

Holi, 23

I

immigration: number of
  Indian Americans, 6, 11, 16

Immigration and Nationality
  Act of 1965, 15

Immigration Act of 1990, 16

J

Jindal, Bobby, 28

K

karma, 7

Khan, Naeem, 29

L

Lazarus, Emma, 13

M

marriage, 21

N

Nadella, Satya, 17

Nooyi, Indra, 27

R

religion(s), 5, 7, 16

S

sari, 21, 25

Sikh, 7, 22, 27

Statue of Liberty, 13

T

Taj Mahal, 9

Y

yoga, 23